# Hands of Healing

# Hands of Healing

A Daily Devotional with Poetry Meditations and Grief Journal

by Martha W. Brandt

Brandt Press
Beverly, Massachusetts

Copyright © 2017 by Brandt Press, Beverly, Massachusetts

All rights reserved. This book or any portion thereof may not be reproduced or used in any manner whatsoever without the express written permission of the publisher except for the use of brief quotations in a book review. Printed in the United States of America.

ISBN 978-0-9992959-0-8

www.marthawbrandt.com

Dedicated to my sister, Karen May Wonson Stearns,
otherwise affectionately known as DeeDee to me and to all her loved ones.

# Introduction

The submission of Hands of Healing is a culmination of my own poetry, as well as motivational, inspirational, and healing words from around the world. My poetry was inspired by the untimely death of my dear sister, Karen May Wonson Stearns (DeeDee), in 2013.

My hope is that the poems and passages will allow others who are grieving to record their own thoughts and desires for spiritual peace and well-being each day. The template is conveniently set up to journal for 365 days (with additional pages at the end of the book) and can be reviewed or rewritten year after year.

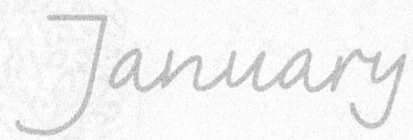

**Oh, To Love Fully**

The beauty in creativity
is like a flower
eager to bloom
shoot forth          discovery

So it is with God's all encompassing love
Its eagerness to warm our hearts
fill our entire being until
we must share this love abundance
with others     like us       yearning

We seek each other to embrace
a child's small hand caress and gentle kiss
a warm hug
letting it linger
feeling its power deep in our soul

Too often we dismiss this most basic need
to be loved, caressed, and cared for always
God reaches us in the most loved ways
open our hearts
fill us to overflowing

That we may continue to receive
return God's greatest gift

January 1

*Oh God, open our hearts so that when we use our hands, we open our hands, we touch with healing grace. Amen.* —United Church of Christ Lenten Handbook

## My Healing Words

January 2

*God did extraordinary miracles through Paul, so that when the handkerchiefs or aprons that had touched his skin were brought to the sick, their diseases left them and the evil spirits came out of them.* —Acts 19:11 (NKJV)

MY HEALING WORDS

January 3

*Dear Lord, fill me with your grace and healing that I may lead the life you have deemed worthy for me.* —Martha W. Brandt

## My Healing Words

January 4

*He reached down from on high and took hold of me; he drew me out of deep waters. He rescued me.* —Psalm 18:16–17 (NKJV)

## My Healing Words

January 5

*How God anointed Jesus of Nazareth with the Holy Spirit and power, and how he went around doing good and healing all who were under the power of the devil because God was with him.* —Acts 10:38 (NKJV)

MY HEALING WORDS

January 6

*Be transformed by the renewing of your mind.* —Romans 12:2 (NIV)

## My Healing Words

January 7

*Jesus is my Savior and Healer. Through him and our dear Lord, all things are possible.* —Martha W. Brandt

## My Healing Words

January 8

*I live now not with my own life but with the life of Christ who lives in me.*
—Galatians 2:20 (NIV)

## My Healing Words

January 9

*And hope does not disappoint us, because God has poured out his love into our hearts by the Holy Spirit, whom he has given us.* —Romans 5:5 (NKJV)

## My Healing Words

January 10

*Evoking the presence of great compassion, let us fill our hearts with our own compassion—toward ourselves and towards all living beings.* —Buddhist Prayer

## My Healing Words

January 11

*Let us pray that all living beings realize that they are all brothers and sisters, all nourished from the same source of life.* —Buddhist Prayer

## My Healing Words

January 12

*The ordinary moves to the extraordinary when we channel the touch of God with our own hands and clothing.* —Anonymous

## My Healing Words

January 13

*Healing happens from the open heart.* —Anonymous

## My Healing Words

January 14

*As long as our touches are small, even domestic, we too can provide miracles of healing.* —Anonymous

MY HEALING WORDS

January 15

*O Lord my God, I cried to you for help, and you have healed me.*
—Psalms 30:2 (NKJV)

## My Healing Words

January 16

*I live now not with my own life but with the life of Christ who lives in me.*
—Galatians 2:20 (NKJV)

## My Healing Words

January 17

*In the same way, the Spirit helps us in our weakness. We do not know what we ought to pray for but the Spirit himself intercedes for us with groans that words cannot express. And he who searches our hearts knows the mind of the Spirit, because the Spirit intercedes for the saints in accordance to God's will.*
—Romans 8:26–27 (NKJV)

## My Healing Words

January 18

*We are what we think. All that we are arises with our thoughts. With our thoughts, we make and heal the world.* —Buddhist Prayer

## My Healing Words

January 19

*Delight yourself also in the Lord and he shall give you the desires of your heart.*
—Psalms 37:4 (NKJV)

## My Healing Words

January 20

*To another faith by the same Spirit, to another gifts of healings by the same Spirit.* —1 Corinthians 12:9 (NKJV)

## My Healing Words

January 21

*With understanding and loving-kindness, we will look within ourselves. We will find healing, happiness, wisdom and serenity.* —Buddhist Prayer

## My Healing Words

January 22

*Give her the fruit of her hands; and let her own works praise her in the gates.*
—Proverbs 31:31 (NKJV)

## My Healing Words

January 23

*And he took them up in his arms, put his hands upon them and blessed them.*
—Mark 10:16 (NKJV)

My Healing Words

January 24

*Be aware of the contact between your feet and the earth. Walk as if you are kissing the earth with your feet. We have caused a lot of damage to the Earth. Now it is time for us to take good care of her. We bring our peace and calm to the surface of the Earth and share the lesson of love. We walk in that healing spirit.* —Thich Nhat Hanh

## My Healing Words

January 25

*May all beings everywhere be happy, peaceful and free. Display a heart of boundless love for all the world.* —Buddhist Prayer

## MY HEALING WORDS

January 26

*And the whole multitude sought to touch Him, for power went out from Him and healed them all.* —Luke 6:19 (NKJV)

## My Healing Words

January 27

*Of the doctrine of baptisms, and of laying on of hands, and of resurrection of the dead, and of eternal judgment.* —Hebrews 6:2 (NKJV)

## My Healing Words

January 28

*Do not dwell in the past. Do not dream of the future. Concentrate the mind on the present moment.* —Buddhist Prayer

## My Healing Words

January 29

*And he led them out as far as to Bethany, and he lifted up his hands, and blessed them.* —Luke 24:50 (NKJV)

My Healing Words

January 30

*May the sun bring you new energy by day. May the moon softly restore you by night. May the rain wash away your worries. May the breeze blow new strength into your being. May you walk gently through the world and know its beauty all the days of your life.* —Apache Blessing

## My Healing Words

January 31

*Have mercy on me, O Lord, for I am weak; O Lord, heal me, for my bones are troubled.* —Psalms 6:2 (NKJV)

## My Healing Words

## February

**Seasoned Grace**

Twenty more inches of snow
I think
I cannot possibly
go forward

The proud, ridiculous bird
sits atop the dune of snow
I creep precariously
across the pavement beach

Is it safe to go?
I inch forward
my neck a crane
of tension, hesitation

But, whizzing by, a car
I stop miraculously
my heart
a pulsing beat of fear, throbbing

I do not see the squirrel
scamper to safety
beyond my car wheel's tread

It is tree-burning day
West Beach
a summer frolic paradise
now burdened
with a bonfire's worth
of spent Christmas trees
at the heaping snow encrusted tides edge

The summer people
now huddled by a booming
crackling, wonderful
fire
cumbersome in coats heavy,
gloves, hats drawn tight

We all delight
in the dancing flames
Taunting our imagination
of sand castles,
the beckoning waves
blazen sun of summer
kissing, caressing
the bare skin

We leave the fire
remnants
My daughter and I
trek boldly forward
the darkness envelopes us
a luxurious cloak
The looming beach in winter
takes us home

We are silent
The waves leave mirrored sand
our footprints a welcome
pattern of life

Together we gaze longingly
stars above bright
with artic blast
close enough to grasp
We are infinitely small
insignificant
but, our breath is one with this vast
universe

We cherish
this dormant time of winter
for in the cold
lies these possibilities
close warmth, connection
amazing love and awe

Quiet in our thoughts
that comfortable space,
a gentle reminder
we are one

The path
illuminated by glitter moonlight,
Snow awash with temptress delight
we can see our footprints
together, intertwined
gratitude envelopes my soul

God has tasked me
to claim delight
in daughters and
New England snow

February 1

*Dear God, help me to see the beauty in my body and to find peace and healing in my soul.* —Martha W. Brandt

## My Healing Words

February 2

*I will not keep silent. I will not rest until the promises of God are fulfilled.*
—Isaiah 62:1 (NKJV)

## My Healing Words

February 3

*And God wrought special miracles by the hands of Paul.* —Acts 19:11 (NKJV)

My Healing Words

February 4

*I do not understand my own actions. For I do not do what I want, but I do the very thing I hate.* —Romans 7:15 (NKJV)

## My Healing Words

February 5

*Do not dwell in the past. Do not dream of the future. Concentrate the mind on the present moment.* —Buddhist Prayer

## My Healing Words

February 6

*May all I say and all I think be in harmony with thee, God within me, God beyond me.* —Chinook Prayer, Pacific Northwest Coast, North America

## My Healing Words

February 7

*All that we are arises with our thoughts. With our thoughts, we make the world.*
—Buddhist Prayer

## My Healing Words

February 8

*Grandfather, sacred one, teach us love, compassion and honor that we may heal the earth and heal each other.* —Ojibway Prayer

## My Healing Words

February 9

*Then your light shall break forth like the morning. Your healing shall spring forth speedily, and your righteousness shall go before you; the glory of the Lord shall be your rear guard.* —Isaiah 58:8 (NKJV)

## My Healing Words

February 10

*By stretching out your hand to heal, and that signs and wonders may be done through the name of your holy servant Jesus Christ.* —Acts 4:30 (NKJV)

## My Healing Words

February 11

*I will try to think pure and beautiful thoughts, to say pure and beautiful words, and to do pure and beautiful deeds, knowing that on what I do now depends my happiness and misery. May every link in Lord Buddha's golden chain of love become bright and strong and may we all attain perfect peace.*
—Buddhist Prayer

## My Healing Words

February 12

*Water flows over these hands. May I use them skillfully to preserve our precious planet.* —Thich Nhat Hahn

MY HEALING WORDS

February 13

*Now when the sun was setting, all they that had any sick with divers diseases brought them unto him; and he laid his hands on every one of them, and healed them.* —Luke 4:40 (NKJV)

## My Healing Words

February 14

*My child, be attentive to my words; incline your ear to my sayings. Do not let them escape from your sight; keep them within your heart. For they are life to those who find them, and healing to all their flesh.* —Proverbs 4:20–22 (NKJV)

MY HEALING WORDS

February 15

*May all beings be peaceful. May all beings be happy. May all beings be safe. May all beings awaken to the light of their true nature. May all beings be free.*
—Metta Prayer

## My Healing Words

February 16

*Neglect not the gift that is in thee, which was given thee by prophecy, with the laying on of the hands of the presbytery.* —1 Timothy 4:14 (NKJV)

## My Healing Words

February 17

*We reverently pray for eternal harmony in the universe. May the weather be seasonable, may the harvest be fruitful, may countries exist in harmony, and may all people enjoy happiness.* —Buddhist Prayer

## My Healing Words

February 18

*If we are peaceful, if we are happy, we can smile and blossom like a flower. Everyone in our family, our entire society will benefit from our peace.*
—Thich Nhat Hanh

## My Healing Words

February 19

*Now when the woman saw that she was not hidden, she came trembling; and falling down before Him, she declared to Him in the presence of all the people the reason she had touched Him and how she was healed immediately.*
—Luke 8:47 (NKJV)

## My Healing Words

February 20

*The spirit of the Lord God is upon me, because the Lord has anointed me to preach good tidings to the poor; he has sent me to heal the brokenhearted. To proclaim liberty to the captives, and the opening of the prison to those who are bound.* —Isaiah 61:1 (NKJV)

## My Healing Words

February 21

*And when Jesus went out he saw a great multitude; and he was moved with compassion for them, and healed their sick.* —Matthew 14:14 (NKJV)

## My Healing Words

February 22

*There is nothing more worthy than the virtue of selflessness. Selflessness unites people. It is a healing herb that unifies strangers and brings families together. It is the love for others that is higher than self-love; it is our only hope.*
—Buddhist Prayer

## MY HEALING WORDS

February 23

*And now may the God of hope fill you with all joy and peace in believing, that you may abound in hope, through the power of the Holy Spirit.*
—Romans 15:13 (NKJV)

## My Healing Words

February 24

*To keep the body in good health is a duty. . . . Otherwise we shall not be able to keep our mind strong and clear.* —Buddhist Prayer

## My Healing Words

February 25

*Be a breath of life unto the body of humankind a dew upon the human heart, and a fruit upon the tree of humility.* —Baha'I Prayer

## My Healing Words

February 26

*For you are one who does not hesitate to respond to our call, you are the cornerstone of peace.* —Native African Prayer

MY HEALING WORDS

February 27

*Love your enemies, do good to those who hate you, bless those who curse you, pray for those who abuse you. Blessed be the Peacemakers, for they shall be called the Children of God.* —Traditional Christian Prayer

MY HEALING WORDS

February 28

*Peace and universal love is the essence of all the teachings. Forgive do I creatures all, and let all creatures forgive me.* —Jain Prayer

## My Healing Words

February 29

*When you realize how perfect everything is you will tilt your head back and laugh at the sky!* —Buddhist Prayer

## My Healing Words

# March

**Dream Baby (2)**

I thought of you today
My dream baby
Now angel and comforter

I am saddened
with the thought
I will never comfort you

**The Awakening**

It is late and dusk descends
My boys and girl begin the rhythmic exhalation of sleep
strong, luxurious, peaceful
Emitting a sense of calm that maddeningly eludes me

While I sing their lullabies and softly touch their sweetness
my heart speaks a multitude
joy, sorrow, grief, healing
and the clocks continue to chime their relentless cry of passing time

I am drawn to the birch beyond my window
the new leaf buds awakening to the call of spring
curling, not quite touching, whispering
They reach for me, I yearn for their emotionless freedom

Soulful searching begins when fatigued emotions relinquish their grip
It is not enough to know certain endings are blessed
emptiness, aching, longing
Clinging to the past cannot propel a soul to its anointed destination

If I press my hand against the sonogram, will her tiny hand feel its
tender touch?
"yes, yes," beckons the wise birch
Will her delicate crossed legs and feet feel the softness of my lips
as I drape them with a final kiss?
"yes, yes," a broken heart weeps

Can I retreat to winter and hibernate there?
I cannot run the many miles this grief chasm consumes
bottomless, unforgiving, life depleting
My path chosen is not this one; What is the purpose?
Where are the plans, the map, the contentment?

The love trick is not what is lost, but what remains
two precious boys and cherubic girl mesmerized with sleep
unaware, unencumbered, fragile
It is simply an ending forging a new beginning
The birch whispers, the children stir, my soul awakens to renewed life,
renewed love

March 1

*Then Jesus said to the centurion, go your way; and as you have believed, so let it be done for you. And his servant was healed that same hour.*
—Matthew 8:13 (NKJV)

## My Healing Words

March 2

*Rise up, my love, my fair one, and come away. For lo, the winter is past, the rain is over and gone.* —The Song of Solomon 2:10–14 (NKJV)

## My Healing Words

March 3

*In the silence of love, you will find the spark of life.* —Rumi

## My Healing Words

March 4

*All are nothing but flowers in a flowing universe.* —Nakagawa Soen-Roshi

## My Healing Words

March 5

*And he said to her, Daughter, be of good cheer, your faith has made you well. Go in peace.* —Luke 8:48 (NKJV)

My Healing Words

March 6

*Peace comes from within. Do not seek it without.* —Buddha

## My Healing Words

March 7

*She aspires to be a tree of life to those who lay hold of her; those who hold her fast are called to be happy.* —Proverbs 3:18 (adapted from NKJV)

MY HEALING WORDS

March 8

*The secret of change is to focus all of your energy, not on fighting the old, but on building the new.* —Socrates

## My Healing Words

March 9

*My heart and my flesh sing with joy to thee, Oh God of life.* —Chinook Psalter

## MY HEALING WORDS

March 10

*Birth and death are present in every moment.* —Thich Nhat Hanh

## My Healing Words

March 11

*Everything that has a beginning has an ending. Make your peace with that and all will be well.* —Buddha

## My Healing Words

March 12

*Simple pleasures are the best, Godly riches while you rest.* —Martha W. Brandt

## My Healing Words

March 13

*God's mighty healing power fills me now. I am whole, well and free.*
—Martha W. Brandt

## My Healing Words

March 14

*God's loving presence within is my guiding light. I make wise choices.*
—Martha W. Brandt

## MY HEALING WORDS

March 15

*Know that we find God when we love, and only that victory endures in consequences of which no one is defeated.* —Sikh Prayer

MY HEALING WORDS

March 16

*Oh God, lead us from the unreal to the real, from darkness to light, from death to immortality. God's peace, peace, peace to all.* —Hindu Prayer

## My Healing Words

March 17

*And the hand of the Lord was with them; and a great number believed, and turned unto the Lord.* —Acts 11:21 (NKJV)

## My Healing Words

March 18

*The breezes at dawn have secrets to tell you. Don't go back to sleep! You must ask for what you really want.* —Rumi

## My Healing Words

March 19

*I vow to live fully in each moment and to look at all beings with eyes of compassion.* —Thich Nhat Hanh

## My Healing Words

March 20

*Let there be long breath and life. Listen to us Father. We ask for good thoughts, heart, love, happiness.* —Arapaho Grace

## My Healing Words

March 21

*From all that dwells below the skies, let faith and hope with joy arise.*
—Unitarian Prayer

## MY HEALING WORDS

March 22

*O Lord, may we today be touched by Grace, fascinated and moved by this your creation, energized by the power of new growth at work in your world.*
—Chinook Psalter

## My Healing Words

March 23

*The burden is lifted, we are free.* —Ancient Hawaiin Healing Chant

MY HEALING WORDS

March 24

*God keep my remembrance pure, God fill my heart with love.* —Chinook Psalter

## My Healing Words

March 25

*Student—How may I enter the Way? Teacher—Do you hear the murmur of the mountain stream? There you may enter.* —Zen Koan

## My Healing Words

March 26

*May we move beyond viewing this life only through a frame, but touch it and be touched by it.* —Chinook Psalter

## My Healing Words

March 27

*He heals the brokenhearted and binds up their wounds.* —Psalms 147:3 (NKJV)

MY HEALING WORDS

March 28

*Life was wonderful and I still feel joy each time the daybreak whitens the dark sky, each time the sun climbs over the roof of the sky.* —Eskimo Song

MY HEALING WORDS

March 29

*To everything there is a season, a time for every purpose under heaven, a time to heal . . .* —Ecclesiastes 3 (NKJV)

My Healing Words

March 30

*Rise up my love, my fair one and come away, for lo, the winter is past, the rain is over and gone.* —Song of Solomon 2:10–14 (NKJV)

## My Healing Words

March 31

*Heal me, O LORD, and I shall be healed; Save me, and I shall be saved, For You are my praise.* —Jeremiah 17:14 (NKJV)

MY HEALING WORDS

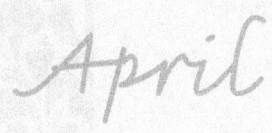

### Boston Strong, Wicked Strong

A pressure cooker
fabricated with stainless steel
most likely
cooks divinely
The heavy metal release valve
whistles
The hot steam can burn
but is necessary for the pressure
relief

A pressure cooker
filled with fabricated
sharp nails
dense ball bearings
release valve absent
weighted in a gray
unassuming backpack
left amidst
marathon revelers

Memories of a marathon past
my family positioned
at the finish line
cheering for me, my first marathon attempt
eerily close
to the pressure cooker backpack
placed at the lamp post
10 years later

Marathon running
the dynamics of movement
a true miracle of motion
like well-worn gears
The joints move in rhythm
to the pounding of pavement

Each breath is rhythmically challenged
feeding the burning lungs
heart pumping, muscles tightening
The mind a guide for each action
a temple of triumph and fortitude

It is at mile 26 with air escaping
calves a spasm of screaming reticence
Exhaustion blankets the body in its purest form
A buddy behind approaches, an earthly angel
guiding, cheering, consoling, comforting

Baby steps, baby steps
forward motion the only option
Seeking landmarks, signifying completion, closure
The raw beauty of this body's perpetual movement
lingers a moment longer
Euphoria fills this weary runner's soul

The blast at the finish line
a contradiction
robbing many runners the ultimate satisfaction
This once safe haven now home to
runners, spectators wounded
Killed
Celebration confused with chaos

A glorious, joyous day
ends in tragedy
Only pieces remain
of the device of destruction
The pressure cooker
serial number
symbolizes brokenness, heart break

But, alas forging forever ahead
with determination and resolve
these bold Bostonians will finish strong

April 1

*I arise today through the strength of heaven.* —Saint Patrick

## My Healing Words

April 2

*Healing doesn't mean the damage never existed. It means the damage no longer controls our lives.* —Akshay Dubey

## My Healing Words

April 3

*All that we are is the result of what we have thought. The mind is everything. What we think we become.* —Buddha

## My Healing Words

April 4

*Do your work, then step back. The only path to serenity.* —Lao Tzu

## My Healing Words

April 5

*Bless the love of the holy one within us.* —Chinook Psalter

## My Healing Words

April 6

*I join my hands in thanks for the many wonders of life.* —Thich Nhat Hanh

MY HEALING WORDS

April 7

*To worry in anticipation or to cherish regret for the past is like the reeds that are cut and wither away.* —Buddha

## My Healing Words

April 8

*I will not let anyone walk through my mind with their dirty feet.*
—Mahatma Ghandi

## MY HEALING WORDS

April 9

*I live now not with my own life but with the life of Christ who lives in me.*
—Galatians 2: 20 (NKJV)

## My Healing Words

April 10

*Remember, remember the sacredness of things.*
—Pawnee, Osage, Omaha Indian Song

## My Healing Words

April 11

*There is no need for suffering, God is here.* —Rumi

## My Healing Words

April 12

*First there must be order and harmony within your own heart. Only then can there be peace and harmony in the world.* —Confucius

MY HEALING WORDS

April 13

*Do not dwell in the past, do not dream of the future, concentrate the mind on the present moment.* —Buddha

## My Healing Words

April 14

*O spirit of the north, purify us with your cleansing, healing winds.*
—Sioux Prayer

## My Healing Words

April 15

*Live your life with great loving-kindness and compassion.* —Buddha

## My Healing Words

April 16

*Please call me by my true names so I can wake up and so the door of my heart can be left open, the door of compassion.* —Thich Nhat Hanh

## My Healing Words

April 17

*I will bless the Lord who guides me; even at night my heart instructs me. I will not be shaken, for he is right beside me.* —Psalm 16:7–8 (NLT)

## My Healing Words

April 18

*Enjoy the blossoms of enlightenment in their season and harvest the fruit of the right path.* —Buddha

## My Healing Words

April 19

*O great spirit, hear me! I am small and weak. I need your strength and wisdom.*
—Traditional Native American Prayer

## My Healing Words

April 20

*May all beings everywhere be happy, peaceful, and free.* —Buddha

## My Healing Words

April 21

*Make me always ready to come to you with clean hands and straight eyes.*
—Traditional Native American Prayer

My Healing Words

April 22

*Don't grieve. Anything you lose comes around in another form.* —Rumi

## My Healing Words

April 23

*And yet, there is only one great thing, the great day that dawns and the light that fills the world.* —Intuit Song

## My Healing Words

April 24

*How wonderful, O Lord, are the works of your hands. The voices of loved ones reveal to us that you are in our midst.* —Jewish Prayer

MY HEALING WORDS

April 25

*And the life that never goes away speaks to me and my heart soars.*
—Navajo Prayer

## My Healing Words

April 26

*As wind carries our prayers for Earth and All Life, may respect and love light our way.* —Tibetan Wind Horse Prayer

## My Healing Words

April 27

*We call upon all that we hold most sacred, the presence and power of the Great Spirit of love and truth and healing.* —Chinook Blessing

MY HEALING WORDS

April 28

*Happily I go forth, impervious to pain, may I walk in beauty; it is finished.*
—Navajo Chant

## My Healing Words

April 29

*In the healing waters, help me here and now.* —Hindu Prayer

## My Healing Words

April 30

*Water flows over these hands. May I use them skillfully to heal.*
—Thich Nhat Hanh

## My Healing Words

### Thin Place

In the darkness of dreams
an angel comes
Clothed in garments old
she softly caresses my face

Speaking without words
a multitude of images . . . . . . . . . . . . clarity
emblazon my being
A story enfolds, a bit of life's
puzzle explained

At birth we were given a blueprint
an imprint on our soul . . . . . . . . . dictating our lifespan
an internal guidance system to find or live
The Question
We are here to learn or find the one question
we are to ask God when we die

The angel leaves me to ponder its significance
I wake refreshed . . . . . . alive . . . . . . . . . . . . energized
to go forth and seek this truth

May 1

*Give us the wisdom to teach our children to love, to respect and to be kind to one another that we may grow with peace of mind.* —Native American Prayer

## My Healing Words

May 2

*May our hearts be filled with compassion for others and ourselves.*
—Tibetan Wind Horse Prayer

## My Healing Words

May 3

*It was the wind that gave them life. It is the wind that comes out of our mouths now that gives us life.* —Navajo Chant

## My Healing Words

May 4

*Healing waters, you are the ones who bring us the life force. Help us to find nourishment so that we may look upon great joy.* —Hindu Prayer

## My Healing Words

May 5

*May peace increase on Earth. May it begin with me.*
—Tibetan Wind Horse Prayer

## My Healing Words

May 6

*Great ones above and below, bless us, for we reach up to you.* —Chinook Psalter

## My Healing Words

May 7

*That from which we draw the healing water of life, here I give unto you your strong spirit.* —Egyptian Prayer

## My Healing Words

May 8

*My joy is like spring, so warm it makes flowers bloom in all walks of life. My pain is like a river of tears, so full it fills up the four oceans.* —Thich Nhat Hanh

MY HEALING WORDS

May 9

*Put forth your hand and raise us up.* —Saint Hildegard of Bingen

## My Healing Words

May 10

*You're song, a wished-for song. Go through the ear to the center. Where sky is, where wind, where silent knowing. Put seeds and cover them. Blades will sprout where you do your work.* —Rumi

MY HEALING WORDS

May 11

*May we walk with grace and may the light of the universe shine upon our path.*
—Anonymous

## My Healing Words

May 12

*The miracle is to walk on the green Earth in the present moment, to appreciate the peace and beauty that are available now.* —Thich Nhat Hanh

My Healing Words

May 13

*Once we learn to touch this peace, we will be healed and transformed. It is not a matter of faith; it is a matter of practice.* —Thich Nhat Hanh

## My Healing Words

May 14

*Pray with a right heart and all will be well.* —Martha W. Brandt

## My Healing Words

May 15

*Death leaves a heartache no one can heal, love leaves a memory no one can steal.* —found on a headstone in Ireland

## My Healing Words

May 16

*May your life be like a wildflower, growing freely in the beauty and joy of each day.* —Native American Proverb

## My Healing Words

May 17

*May the longtime sun shine upon you, all love surround you, and the sweet light within you guide your way on.* —Traditional Irish Blessing

## My Healing Words

May 18

*All shall be well and all shall be well and all manner of thing shall be well blessed.* —Julian of Norwich

## My Healing Words

May 19

*We are aware that understanding is the very foundation of love.*
—Thich Nhat Hanh

## My Healing Words

May 20

*Someone fills the cup in front of us. We taste only sacredness.* —Rumi

## My Healing Words

May 21

*God, make me brave, life brings such blinding things. Help me to keep my sight; help me to see aright that out of darkness comes light.* —Author Unknown

## My Healing Words

May 22

*Earth, ourselves, breathe and awaken, leaves are stirring, all things moving, new day coming, life renewing.* —Pawnee Prayer

## My Healing Words

May 23

*Display a heart of boundless love for all the world.* —Buddha

## My Healing Words

May 24

*He giveth power to the faint; and to them that have no might He increaseth strength.* —Isaiah 40:29 (NKJV)

## My Healing Words

May 25

*May all things move and be moved in me and know and be known in me. May all creation dance for joy within me.* —Chinook Psalter

MY HEALING WORDS

May 26

*Lord, we come to you through one another. Lord, we come to you in all our need. Lord, we come to you seeking wholeness. Lay your hands, gently lay your hands.*
—Saint Bernadette

## My Healing Words

May 27

*O, Lord, I come to seek thy shelter: Bless me with thy grace.*
—Sacred Song of the Sikhs

## My Healing Words

May 28

*May the power of every moment of your goodness flow forth to awaken and heal all beings.* —Traditional Buddhist Blessing

## My Healing Words

May 29

*Happiness never decreases by being shared.* —Buddha

## My Healing Words

May 30

*If you speak or act with a calm, bright heart, then happiness follows you, like a shadow that never leaves.* —Buddha

## My Healing Words

May 31

*Embrace all goodness.* —Buddha

## My Healing Words

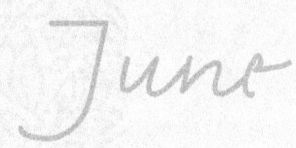

### The Mother, Daughter Dance

I watched my daughter
grow up today
We are navigating the
awkward
moment
from sweet, biddable baby girl
to young adult
stubborn
sometimes sassy
independent young woman

I'm frightened of the transformation
I fear the thought of letting go
but I must do this, reluctantly
She is strengthening
in her resolve
to become her unique self
separate from me

I am in awe of her
becoming such a beautiful, secure soul
I am in awe of her
this part of me I nurtured
for a lifetime
I feel I must perpetuate
the leadership
the knowing
the ultimate involvement
a mother provides to her young

But alas,
in order for the young
to grow and experience
their own desires, falterings
I must let go
A sobering thought
of Motherhood relinquishment
begins the dance
to separation

But not love lost
It is there the truth lies
We are bound together
eternally
in love and approval
My daughter undeniably
part of me
but separate
She will carve her future
out of the love we share

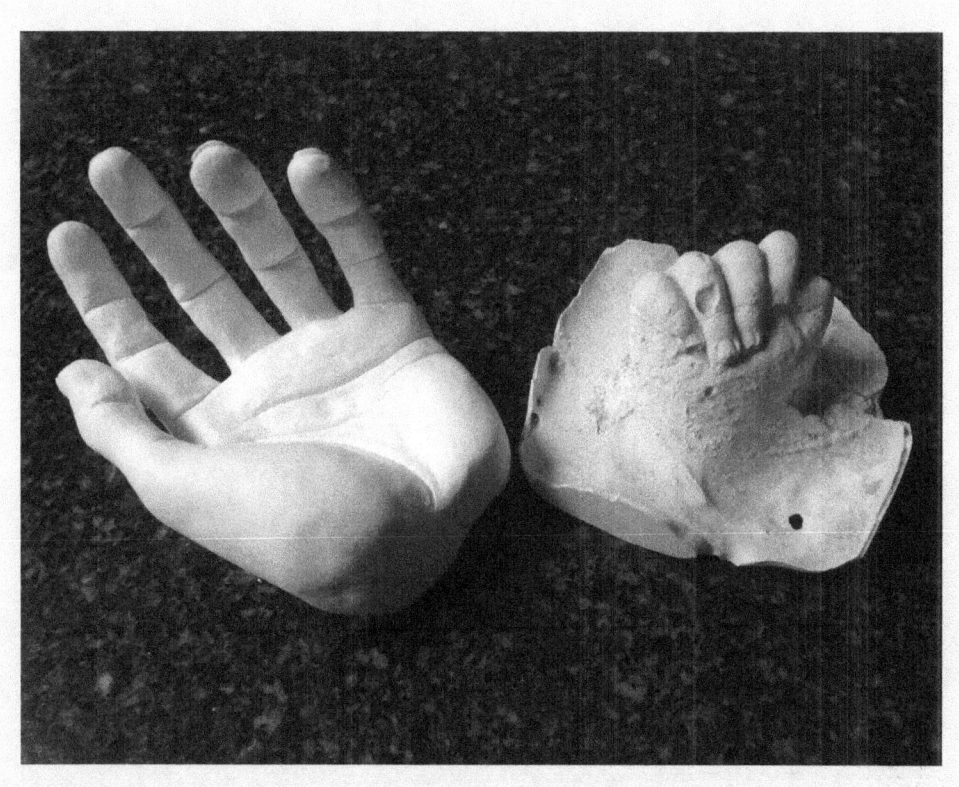

June 1

*Purify the mind and heart to attain happiness. Be kind. Be compassionate.*
—Buddha

## My Healing Words

June 2

*Loving-kindness is giving others happiness. Compassion is removing others' bitterness. Joy is freeing others from suffering.* —Buddha

MY HEALING WORDS

June 3

*Dear God, fill my heart with compassion that I may use gentle hands and kind words for those I love.* —Martha W. Brandt

## My Healing Words

June 4

*Lay your hands gently upon us. Let their touch render your peace, let them bring your forgiveness and healing. Lay your hands, gently lay your hands.*
—Saint Bernadette

## My Healing Words

June 5

*By stretching out your hand to heal, and that signs and wonders may be done through the name of your holy servant Jesus Christ.* —Acts 4:30 (NKJV)

MY HEALING WORDS

June 6

*Now when the sun was setting. All they that had any sick with divers diseases brought them unto him: and he laid his hands on every one of them, and healed them.* —Luke 4:40 (NKJV)

## My Healing Words

June 7

*May all beings be peaceful. May all beings be happy. May all beings be safe. May all beings awaken to the light of their true nature. May all beings be free.*
—Metta Prayer

## MY HEALING WORDS

June 8

*When you realize how perfect everything is you will tilt your head back and laugh at the sky!* —Buddhist Prayer

## My Healing Words

June 9

*O Sacred one, teach us love, compassion and honor that we may heal the earth and each other.* —United Church of Christ Lenten Handbook

My Healing Words

June 10

*May the spark of God's love light the love in my heart, that it may burn brightly through the day.* —Traditional Celtic Prayer

MY HEALING WORDS

June 11

*May you know how to look at yourself with the eyes of understanding and love.*
—Thich Nhat Hanh

## My Healing Words

June 12

*May you learn how to nourish yourself with joy each day.* —Thich Nhat Hanh

MY HEALING WORDS

June 13

*I pray that this day I show forth the divine glory by living a life of creativeness, which shows forth the true individual.* —Shinto Prayer

## My Healing Words

June 14

*A generous heart, kind speech and a life of service and compassion are the things that renew humanity and can heal the world.* —Buddha

MY HEALING WORDS

June 15

*Hold on to my hand, even if I have gone away from you.* —Pueblo Blessing

## My Healing Words

June 16

*For thoughts, words and works, pray we, O God, for forgiveness.*
—Persian Prayer

## My Healing Words

June 17

*Have pity on those who loved each other and were torn apart. Have pity on the loneliness of the heart, on the feebleness of our Faith, on the objects of our tenderness.* —Ancient Prayer of Protection

## My Healing Words

June 18

*Have pity on those who weep, on those who pray, on those who tremble. Give everyone hopefulness and peace.* —Ancient Prayer of Protection

MY HEALING WORDS

June 19

*May beings all live happily and safe and may their hearts rejoice within themselves.* —Buddha

MY HEALING WORDS

June 20

*May God the Holy Spirit move within us and give us eyes to see with, ears to hear with and hands that your work might be done.* —Saint Dominic

## My Healing Words

June 21

*Father, thank you for your revelation about death and illness and sorrow. Your extended arms fill us with joy, expressing love, love caring and carrying, asking and receiving our trust.* —Masai Prayer, Tanzania

## My Healing Words

June 22

*Ask, and it will be given to you; seek, and you will find; knock, and the door will be opened to you. For everyone who asks, receives; and he who seeks, finds; and to him who knocks, the door will be opened.* —Matthew 7:7–8 (NKJV)

## My Healing Words

June 23

*There is a force within that gives you life—seek that.* —Rumi

My Healing Words

June 24

*We call upon all that we hold most sacred, the presence and power of the Great Spirit of love and truth which flows through all the universe to be with us to teach us, and show us the way.* —Chinook Blessing Litany

## MY HEALING WORDS

June 25

*In the breath that I am, I am renewed.* —Jin Shin Jyutsu

## My Healing Words

June 26

*I pray for a day of surprises and unexpected Joy.* —Martha W. Brandt

MY HEALING WORDS

June 27

*May the stars carry your sadness away. May the flowers fill your heart with beauty. May hope forever wipe away your tears and above all, may silence make you strong.* —Native American Blessing

## My Healing Words

June 28

*Be kind whenever possible. It is always possible.* —The Dalai Lama

## My Healing Words

June 29

*May the sun bring you new energy by day. May the moon softly restore you by night. May the rain wash away your worries. May the breeze blow new strength into your being. May you walk gently through the world and know its beauty all the days of your life.* —Apache Blessing

## MY HEALING WORDS

June 30

*Be still and know that I am God.* —Psalm 46:10 (NKJV)

## My Healing Words

### Broken Arrow Wounds

Death is swift
like an arrow
piercing through
the unyielding heart of life

If we are quick enough
side step
bow low
to the depths of our soul
it will miss us
this once

Unaware
we blunder forever forward
to the endless forward we seek
an illusion
infinity
Our soul yearns for the embodiment
of the body
but are we truly free this way?

If a broken arrow
pierces our heart and soul
will we die?

We bless those whose souls
are relinquished
free, unbinding
but we, the living embrace life
shun death and grace
wraps us in its tapestry

In this way we seek truth
seek one another
For love is the greatest seal
for broken arrow wounds

Once we skirt death
the balm of love in our hearts
comforts the soul
to take refuge in the earthly body
for one more blessed day
that the Lord has made
Let us rejoice and be glad in it!

Amen

## Weaving a Net of Prayer

The nets are cast
into the sea of souls
Tiny threads illuminate
the cross-hatch pattern

Woven gently with prayers
colorful images of
want, need, sorrow, gratitude, grace
The myriad of sweeping,
bursts of color and hope
comfort the caregiver
the multitude of weavers

This net of prayer
connects us all
to each other
to the world
Cleanse your spiritual soul
Come sit and pray with me
I tie a thread for you
my beloved

July 1

*And one of them, when he saw that he was healed, returned, and with a loud voice glorified God.* —Luke 17:15 (NKJV)

MY HEALING WORDS

July 2

*In the end only three things matter: how much you loved, how gently you lived and how gracefully you let go of things not meant for you.* —Buddha

## My Healing Words

July 3

*There is no need for suffering, God is here.* —Rumi

## My Healing Words

July 4

*Truly, truly, I say to you, if you ask the Father for anything in my name, he will give it to you.* —John 16:23 (NASB)

## My Healing Words

July 5

*Another day of sun, replenishment and nurturing. Embrace the day and hug yourself a little tighter, for you are worthy of all of its entitlements dear one.*
—Martha W. Brandt

## My Healing Words

July 6

*This is the last world I shall make. I place it in your hands. Hold it in trust.*
—Jewish Prayer

## My Healing Words

July 7

*Oh Great Spirit, I pray for myself in order that I may be healed.* —Navajo Prayer

My Healing Words

July 8

*In the sky, there is no distinction of east and west; people create distinctions out of their own minds and then believe them to be true.* —Buddha

## My Healing Words

July 9

*He sent his word and healed them, and delivered them from their destructions.*
—Psalms 107:20 (NKJV)

## My Healing Words

July 10

*And into my warm body, drawing his breath, I add to your breath that happily you may always live.* —Zuni Chant

MY HEALING WORDS

July 11

*May all I say and all I think be in harmony with thee, God within me, God beyond me.* —Chinook Psalter

### My Healing Words

July 12

*Dear God, I need your help. Please bestow upon me your healing presence and forgive me. Amen.* —Martha W. Brandt

## My Healing Words

July 13

*Quiet yourself and listen for the healing whisper of God in this busy world.*
—Anonymous

## My Healing Words

July 14

*O Lord my God, I cried out to you for help and you healed me.*
—Psalm 30:2 (NKJV)

## My Healing Words

July 15

*Dear God, use my hands to heal the world so that we may live with compassion and loving-kindness.* —Venerable Master Chin Kung

## My Healing Words

July 16

*My heart is a place of prayer.* —Rumi

## My Healing Words

July 17

*Do not say that I'll depart tomorrow because even today I still arrive.*
—Thich Nhat Hanh

## My Healing Words

July 18

*We call to each other, we listen to each other, our hearts deepen with love and compassion.* —Navajo Prayer

## My Healing Words

July 19

*The arch of sky and mightiness of storms encompasses me. I am left trembling with joy.* —Eskimo Song

## My Healing Words

July 20

*Now talking God, your voice speaks for me. Beauty is before me and beauty is behind me. I am surrounded by it. I am immersed in it.*
—Native American Prayer

## MY HEALING WORDS

July 21

*Drink your tea slowly and reverently, as if it is the axis on which the world earth revolves—slowly, evenly, without rushing toward the future. Live the actual moment. Only this moment is life.* —Thich Nhat Hanh

MY HEALING WORDS

July 22

*Is it really so that the one I love is everywhere?* —Rumi

## My Healing Words

July 23

*Fear thou not, for I am with thee; be not dismayed, for I am thy God; I will strengthen thee; yea, I will help thee; yea, I will uphold thee with the right hand of my righteousness.* —Isaiah 41:10 (NKJV)

## My Healing Words

July 24

*Words have the power to both destroy and heal. When words are both true and kind, they can change our world.* —Buddha

## My Healing Words

July 25

*The wailing of broken hearts is the doorway to God.* —Rumi

My Healing Words

July 26

*May we be helped to do here whatever is most right.*
—Traditional American Indian Prayer

## My Healing Words

July 27

*We pray to God that understanding will triumph over ignorance, that generosity will triumph over indifference, that trust will triumph over contempt, and that truth will triumph over falsehood.* —Zoroastrian

## MY HEALING WORDS

July 28

*Behold, I will bring it health and healing; I will heal them and reveal to them the abundance of peace and truth.* —Jeremiah 33:6 (NKJV)

## My Healing Words

July 29

*God, you transform all who are touched by you.* —Rumi

## My Healing Words

July 30

*We bring you gifts that you love. Weave for us a garment of brightness and healing.* —Tewa Pueblo Prayer

## My Healing Words

July 31

*My healing words are tied in one with my body and my heart.*
—Yokuts Indian Prayer

## My Healing Words

*August*

### A Whisper of Love

It is a veil
a thin mask, a whisper of
existence
between life and death

It is there
all around us, always
Wooing those
who listen intently

Feel the need to allow
death's beguiling fingers
stroking
Beckoning us to crossover

The fear keeps us stagnant
Our eyes are blind
Our body defiant
Our soul yearns for the peace

Departing is troublesome
Hindered often by the living love
What torment we experience
letting go of our deepest love
for the soul that must leave
within the whisper of this veiled curtain of death

A deep breath in
and out
It is that close
Thin as air
A whisper of love and hope
eternal

August 1

*Remember, for everything you have lost, you have gained something else. Without the dark, you would never see the stars.* —LiveLifeHappy.com

## My Healing Words

August 2

*I wish Heaven had visiting hours.* —AngelsKeepSake.com

## My Healing Words

August 3

*Live as if you were to die tomorrow. Learn as if you were to live forever.*
—Mahatma Ghandi

## MY HEALING WORDS

August 4

*God promises to make something good out of the storms that bring devastation to your life.* —Romans 8:28 (NKJV)

## My Healing Words

August 5

*Write the wrongs that are done to you in sand, but write the good things that happen to you on a piece of marble. Let go of all emotions such as resentment and retaliation, which diminish you, and hold onto the emotions, such as gratitude and joy, which increase you.* —Arabic Proverb

My Healing Words

August 6

*May all beings have happiness, and the causes of happiness.* —Buddhist Prayer

My Healing Words

August 7

*Be still and know that I am God.* —Psalm 46:10 (NKJV)

## My Healing Words

August 8

*You can only go halfway into the darkest forest; then you are coming out the other side.* —Chinese Proverb

## My Healing Words

August 9

*As long as space endures, as long as there are beings to be found, may I continue likewise to remain to soothe the sufferings of those who live.* —Dalai Lama

## My Healing Words

August 10

*A joy, a depression, a meanness, some momentary awareness comes as an unexpected visitor. Welcome and entertain them all! He may be clearing you out for some new delight.* —Rumi

## My Healing Words

August 11

*After a while you learn the subtle difference between holding a hand and chaining a soul. So you plant your own garden and decorate your own soul.*
—Anonymous

## My Healing Words

August 12

*Our problems are solved by loving-kindness, by gentleness, by joy.* —Buddha

## My Healing Words

August 13

*Loving-kindness can never exist unless it flows from the mind and heart, from understanding and love.* —Buddha

## My Healing Words

August 14

*We are radiant light and sacred dark. The balance.* —Native American

## My Healing Words

August 15

*The arch of sky and mightiness of storms encompass me and I am left trembling with joy.* —Eskimo Song

## My Healing Words

August 16

*Don't grieve. Anything you lose comes around in another form.* —Rumi

## My Healing Words

August 17

*And yet there is only one great thing . . . the great day that dawns and the light that fills the world.* —Inuit Song

## My Healing Words

August 18

*How wonderful, O Lord, are the works of your hands! The heavens declare your glory, the arch of the sky displays your handiwork.* —Jewish Prayer

## My Healing Words

August 19

*Say not in grief, she is no more, but live in thankfulness that she was.*
—Hebrew Proverb

## My Healing Words

August 20

*Today appreciate, be kind, be gentle. Worship your God. Gladden the heart of a child. Take pleasure in the beauty and wonder of the earth. Speak it again. Speak it still again. Speak it still once again.* —Anonymous

## My Healing Words

August 21

*How strong the pain was, but you were stronger. How deep the fall was, but you were even deeper. How dark the night was, but you were the noon day sun in it. You are our father, our mother, our brother and our friend.* —African Prayer

## My Healing Words

August 22

*And let your thoughts spring from love. Born out of concern for all beings.*
—Buddha

## MY HEALING WORDS

August 23

*Endurance, cleanliness, strength, purity will keep our lives straight, our actions only for a good purpose.* —Lakota Sioux Sweat Lodge Ceremony

## My Healing Words

August 24

*Life has meaning only in the struggles. Triumph or defeat is in the hands of God. So let us celebrate the struggles.* —Swahili Warrior Song

## My Healing Words

August 25

*Dear God, lead us from despair to hope, from fear to trust. Let peace and healing fill our hearts.* —Anonymous

## My Healing Words

August 26

*I am the sacred works of the Earth. It is lovely indeed, it is lovely indeed.*
—Song of the Earth Spirit, Navajo Origin Legend

## My Healing Words

August 27

*We belong to the Earth, this we know. We are all connected, like the blood which unites one family. All things are connected.* —Native American

MY HEALING WORDS

August 28

*Do not say that I'll depart tomorrow, because even today I still arrive.*
—Thich Nhat Hanh

## My Healing Words

August 29

*I still arrive, in order to laugh and to cry, in order to fear and to hope. The rhythm of my heart is the birth and death of all that are alive.*
—Thich Nhat Hanh

## My Healing Words

August 30

*Hope is a waking dream.* —Aristotle

## My Healing Words

August 31

*Please call me by my true names, so I can hear all my cries and my laughs at once, so I can see that my joy and pain are one.* —Thich Nhat Hanh

## MY HEALING WORDS

# September

### Life's Fabric: Love

There are only three states of equilibrium
rest, love, death
Death becomes rest becomes love
The final absolute state is love
This is the dance of life

We are all connected by love
a fragile thread
a sacred weave binding us all together
Don't break it or pull it too thin

Its recoil is slow and sad
Its strength is in a gentle touch
a kind word
a thoughtful gaze

Learn how to recognize its power
deep within you, within all of us
yearning to be born
discovered
nourished

A warm flame to be devoured
fueled to perform brave acts of compassion
and care
for all of those dear ones we hold close to
our hearts
They deserve such greatness
endearment

The troubled, broken ones
are hardest to mold
nurture
forgive

Find the love thread
It is everywhere
It is in everyone
waiting for the tight embrace
a relished kiss, a wondrous warmth

The ultimate gift is love
a gift from God
Cherish every moment of loves' blessings
for you to give and receive,
receive and give

Drink its nectar
Feel its power in your being
It is always there in
waiting, wanting, weeping

Trust that love is all there is
and always will be
precious, possible, powerful

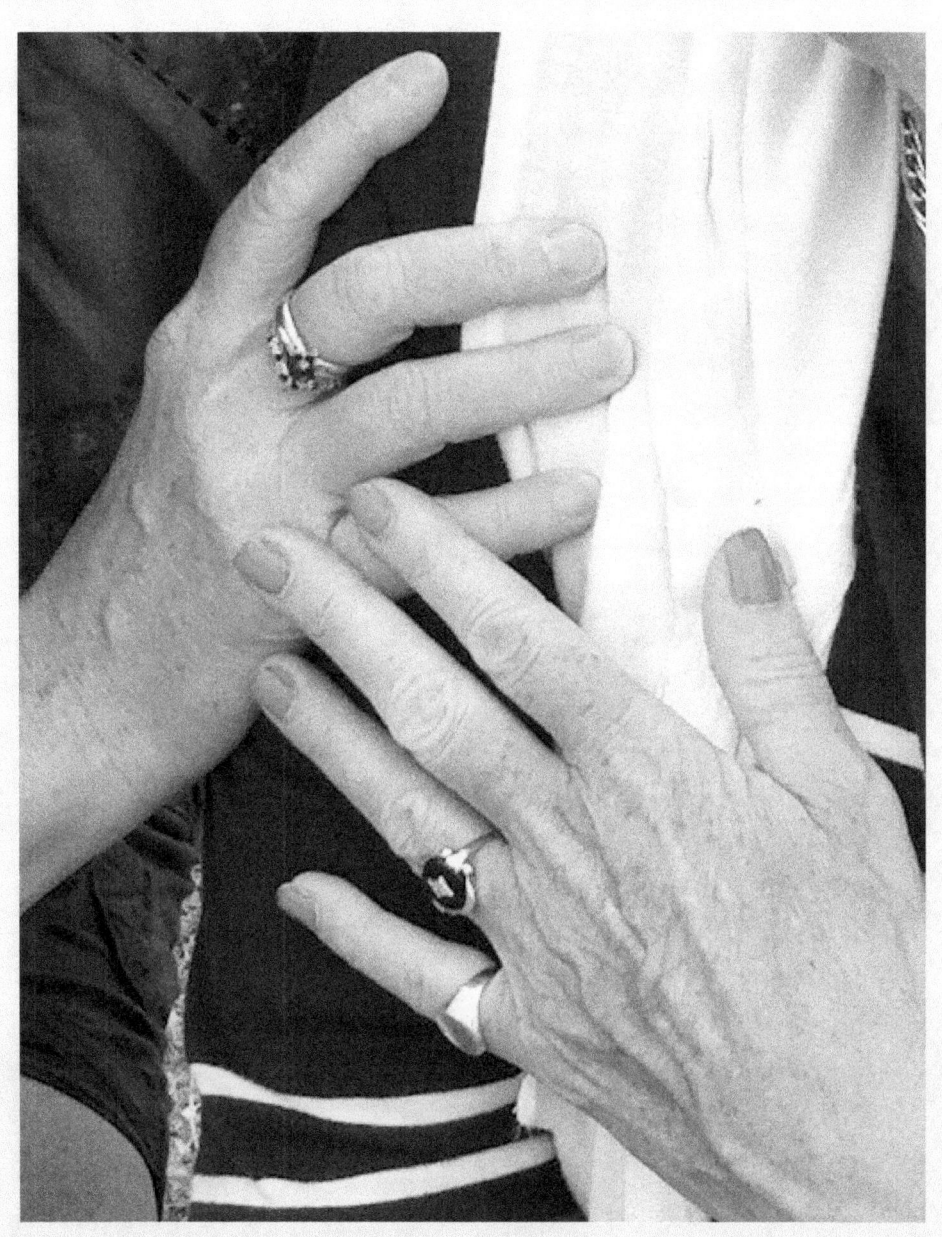

September 1

*Please call me by my names, so I can wake up and so the door of my heart can be left open, the door of compassion.* —Thich Nhat Hanh

## My Healing Words

September 2

*And as you are patient with our struggles to learn, so shall we be patient with ourselves and each other.* —Native American

MY HEALING WORDS

September 3

*Breathe in Grace. Breathe out Gratitude.* —Anonymous

## My Healing Words

September 4

*God is Good. All the time. All the time, God is good.*
—God's Not Dead, the movie

## My Healing Words

September 5

*In the end only three things matter: How much you loved, how gently you lived and how gracefully you let go of things not meant for you.* —Buddha

## My Healing Words

September 6

*In your goodness you have made us able to hear the music of the world. The voices of loved ones reveal to us that you are in our midst. A divine voice sings through all creation.* —Jewish Prayer

MY HEALING WORDS

September 7

*Teach us love, compassion and honor that we may heal the earth and heal each other.* —Ojibway Prayer

## My Healing Words

September 8

*We call upon all that we hold most sacred, the presence and power of the Great Spirit of love and truth which flows through all the universe, to be with us to teach us and show us the way.* —Chinook Blessing Litany

MY HEALING WORDS

September 9

*Happily I recover, happily I go forth. May it be beautiful before me, behind me, below me, above me, all around me. In beauty it is finished.* —Navajo Chant

## My Healing Words

September 10

*Heal me, O Lord, and I shall be healed; Save me, and I shall be saved: for thou art my praise.* —Tanuch/Prophets Jeremiah XVII, 14

## My Healing Words

September 11

*This is how a human being can change. There is a worm addicted to eating grape leaves. Suddenly he wakes up, call it grace, whatever, something wakes him and he's no longer a worm. He's the entire vineyard, and the orchard, too, the fruit, the trunks, a growing wisdom and joy that doesn't need to devour.* —Rumi

## My Healing Words

September 12

*O merciful Father, who has given life to many and lovest all that thou has made, give us the spirit of thine own loving-kindness that we may show mercy to all helpless creatures.* —Traditional Christian Prayer

## My Healing Words

September 13

*Especially would we pray for those which minister to our sport or comfort that they may be treated with tenderness of hands, in thankfulness of heart, and that we may discover thee, the Creator, in all created things.*
—Traditional Christian Prayer

## My Healing Words

September 14

*As the sun illuminates the moon and the stars, so let us illumine one another.*
—Anonymous

## My Healing Words

September 15

*Keep on praying for the thing that you are waiting for.* —Anonymous

## My Healing Words

September 16

*God is good, God is good, God is good, He is so good to me. He cares for me, He cares for me, He cares for me, He is so good to me.*
—Traditional Christian Prayer

## My Healing Words

September 17

*Heavenly Father, charge my body with Thy vitality, charge my mind with Thy spiritual power, charge my soul with Thy joy, Thine immortality.*
—Yogananda, Metaphysical Meditations

## My Healing Words

September 18

*Let not your hearts be troubled, neither let them be afraid.* —John 14:27 (NKJV)

## My Healing Words

September 19

*Make us worthy, Lord, to serve others throughout the world who live and die in poverty or hunger, give them, through our hands, this day their daily bread, and by our understanding love, give peace and joy.* —Mother Teresa

## My Healing Words

September 20

*Bless all people; pray for their happiness, joy and laughter.* —Vedic Scriptures

## My Healing Words

September 21

*Enable me so to live that I may daily do something to lessen the tide of human sorrow, and add to the sum of human happiness.* —Traditional Christian Prayer

MY HEALING WORDS

September 22

*Water flows over these hands may I use them skillfully to preserve our precious planet.* —Thich Nhat Hanh

## My Healing Words

September 23

*O powers above us, bless us with your gifts, for we reach up to you.*
—Chinook Psalter

## My Healing Words

September 24

*Spirit of God in the clear running water, blowing to greatness the trees on the hill, Spirit of God in the finger of morning fill the earth, bring it to birth and blow where you will. Blow, blow, blow till I be but breath of the spirit blowing in me.* —East African Medical Missionary Sisters

## My Healing Words

September 25

*May all I say and think be in harmony with thee, God within me, God beyond me.* —Chinook Psalter

## My Healing Words

September 26

*Listen to the wind, it talks. Listen to the silence, it speaks. Listen to your heart, it knows.* —Native American Proverb

## My Healing Words

September 27

*For the wounds, but he binds up; he shatters, but his hands heal.*
—Job 5:18 (ESV)

## My Healing Words

September 28

*Now when the sun was setting, all those who had any who were sick with various diseases brought them to him, and he laid his hands on every one of them and healed them.* —Luke 4:40 (ESV)

My Healing Words

September 29

*Today, today, today, bless us and help us to grow.* —Rosh Hashanah Liturgy

## My Healing Words

September 30

*Evening and morning, and at noon will I pray, and cry aloud: and he shall hear my voice.* —Psalm 55:17 (NKJV)

## My Healing Words

*October*

### Within Grief Transcends Delight

I lost my way to the spirit
the path had become overgrown
with muddied, gnarled
fingers of fear
clenching my heart
seizing my soul

Gasping for breath
I seek solace in numbness
loss of feeling
is safe
secure
Relentless in its absence
of delight

A loved one lost
creates chasms of grief
overwhelming
Too powerful to invite
Delight

My daily walks
in joyful summer glow
have become burnished bronze
cool, crisp
A stark reminder
of season's end
Soul sisters' separation

I weep for you, dear one
but today the October sun
warmed my face
just enough
to remind me
where a butterfly
not too long ago
fleetingly kissed
my cheek

A divine gift
of her spirit
welcoming delight

October 1

*May everyone be happy and safe, and may their hearts be filled with joy.*
—Thich Nhat Hanh

## My Healing Words

October 2

*Follow diligently the way in your own heart, but make no display of it to the world. Keep behind, and you shall be put in front; keep out, and you shall be kept in. He that humbles himself shall be preserved entire. He that bends shall be made straight. He that is empty shall be filled. He that is worn out shall be renewed.* —Lao Tzu

## My Healing Words

October 3

*God declares: I think of you and I have plans for you, prosperity and a future filled with hope.* —Jeremiah 29:11 (NKJV)

## My Healing Words

October 4

*O God, who by the grace of the Holy Ghost hast poured the gifts of love into our hearts; Grant unto my friends and kindred, health of body and soul, and every spiritual gift, that they may love thee with all their strength, and with perfect affection fulfill thy pleasure!* —Traditional Christian Prayer

## My Healing Words

October 5

*May the spark of God's love light the love in my heart, that it may burn brightly through the day.* —Traditional Celtic Prayer

## My Healing Words

October 6

*Do your work, then step back. The only path to serenity.* —Lao Tzu

## My Healing Words

October 7

*O God, who by the grace of the Holy Ghost hast poured the gifts of love into our hearts; Grant unto my friends and kindred, health of body and soul, and every spiritual gift, that they may love thee with all their strength, and with perfect affection fulfill thy pleasure!* —Traditional Christian Prayer

## My Healing Words

October 8

*Live blamelessly; God is present.* —Author unknown

## My Healing Words

October 9

*Holy Spirit, giving life to all life, moving all creatures, root of all things washing them clean, wiping out their mistakes, healing their wounds, you are our true life, luminous, wonderful, awakening the heart from its ancient sleep.*
—Hildegard of Bingen

## My Healing Words

October 10

*They said, if you send away the ark of the God of Israel, do not send it empty, but by all means return him a guilt offering. Then you will be healed, and it will be known to you why his hand does not turn away from you.*
—1 Samuel 6:3 (ESV)

## My Healing Words

October 11

*Whatever house I enter, I shall come to heal.* —Hippocratic Oath

## My Healing Words

October 12

*Hear our humble prayer, O God, for our friends the animals. We entreat for them all thy mercy and pity, and for those who deal with them we ask a heart of compassion and gentle hands and kindly words.* —Russian Prayer

## My Healing Words

October 13

*I come before thee as one of thy many children. See, I am small and weak; I need thy strength and wisdom.* —Sioux Prayer

## My Healing Words

October 14

*Make me ever ready to come to thee with pure hands and candid eyes, so that my spirit, when life disappears like the setting sun, may stand unashamed before thee.* —Sioux Prayer

## My Healing Words

October 15

*O Great Spirit, make me always ready to come to you with clean hands and straight eyes.* —Traditional Native American Prayer

## My Healing Words

October 16

*And he could do no mighty work there, except that he laid his hands on a few sick people and healed them.* —Mark 6:5 (ESV)

## My Healing Words

October 17

*And a man was there with a withered hand. And they asked him, Is it lawful to heal on the Sabbath? So that they might accuse him.* —Matthew 12:10 (ESV)

My Healing Words

October 18

*Bless the wisdom of the Holy One above us, bless the truth of the Holy One beneath us, bless the love of the Holy One within us.* —Chinook Psalter

## My Healing Words

October 19

*Grandfather Great Spirit, fill us with the light. Give us the strength to understand, and the eyes to see. Teach us to walk the soft earth as relatives to all that live.* —Sioux Prayer

## My Healing Words

October 20

*O Great Spirit, make my hands respect the things you have made and my ears sharp to hear your voice.* —Traditional Native American Prayer

My Healing Words

October 21

*See now that I, even I, am he, and there is no god beside me; I kill and I make alive; I wound and I heal; and there is none that can deliver out of my hand.*
—Deuteronomy 32:39 (ESV)

## MY HEALING WORDS

October 22

*We return thanks to the Great Spirit, in whom is embodied all goodness, and who directs all things for the good of his children.* —Iroquois Prayer (adapted)

## My Healing Words

October 23

*Waking up this morning, I see blue sky. I join my hands in thanks for the many wonders of life.* —Thich Nhat Hanh

## My Healing Words

October 24

*Be praised my Lord for those who pardon by your love and suffer illness and grief. Bless those who undergo in silence the poor for whom you hold a crown.*
—Saint Francis of Assisi

## My Healing Words

October 25

*O praise my Lord and bless my Lord and thank and serve my Lord with humbleness Triumphant.* —Saint Francis of Assisi

## My Healing Words

October 26

*Our hands are powerful healers.* —Martha W. Brandt

## My Healing Words

October 27

*To everything there is a season . . . a time to heal.* —Ecclesiastes 3: 1-8, LAMSA

## My Healing Words

October 28

*Life was wonderful and I still feel joy each time the daybreak whitens the dark sky and each time the sun climbs over the roof of the sky.* —Eskimo Song

## My Healing Words

October 29

*Oh sweet bitterness! I will soothe you and heal you.* —Rumi

My Healing Words

October 30

*While you stretch out your hand to heal, and signs and wonders are performed through the name of your holy servant Jesus.* —Acts 4:30 (ESV)

My Healing Words

October 31

*It happened that the father of Publius lay sick with fever and dysentery. And Paul visited him and prayed, and putting his hands on him healed him.*
—Acts 28:8 (ESV)

## My Healing Words

# November

**Labyrinth**

I sit alone in silence
gazing outside my window
I see jeweled drops of water
likened to tears
The tree branches heavy laden
with their crystal burden
the rain is melodic, soothing
I let go and open my heart, my soul
to God's whisper of nourishment
love and grace

It is this spiritual journey that
weaves blasts of beauty, awe, love,
pain, grief, loss
into a mosaic of true self and rightness
Skirting the edges, side-stepping,
opportunities lost, avoided
do not alter the forward momentum

The center calls,
a lost soul senses freedom
a gentle nudging, the powerful presence
It is here God directs and molds
our beautiful beings
timeless
true

We seek direction
the way in is the way out
All journeys begin and end and begin again
We are not complete
We rejoice in the eternal energy
the assurance of peace and purpose

How blessed are we to be enveloped
by so many who love and are forever loved
A grateful day indeed
to journey together
we spirited and very special women!!

November 1

*Oh Lord, may we today be touched by grace, fascinated and moved by this your creation, energized by the power of new growth at work in your world.*
—Chinook Psalter

## My Healing Words

November 2

*The breezes at dawn have secrets to tell you. Don't go back to sleep! You must ask for what you really want. Don't go back to sleep!* —Rumi

## My Healing Words

November 3

*God keep my remembrance pure. God fill my heart with love and may my prayer be beautiful.* —Chinook Psalter

## My Healing Words

November 4

*O Lord, may we move beyond viewing this life only through a frame, but touch it and be touched by it. Know it and be known by it. Love it and be loved by it.*
—Chinook Psalter

## My Healing Words

November 5

*The smallest hands are the most powerful healers.* —Martha W. Brandt

## My Healing Words

November 6

*When you like a flower, you just pluck it. But when you love a flower, you water it daily. One who understands this, understands life.* —Buddha

## My Healing Words

November 7

*Arise, O Lord; O God, lift up thy hand; forget not the afflicted.*
—Psalm 10:12 (RSV)

## My Healing Words

November 8

*Holy persons draw to themselves all that is earthly.* —Hildegard of Bingen

My Healing Words

November 9

*When you walk across the fields with your mind pure and holy, then from all the stones, and all growing things, and all animals, the sparks of their souls come out and cling to you, and then they are purified and become a holy fire in you.*
—Hasidic Saying

## My Healing Words

November 10

*In his hand are the depths of the earth: the heights of the mountains are his also.*
—Psalm 95:4 (RSV)

## My Healing Words

November 11

*Eagle soaring, see the morning, see the new mysterious morning, something marvelous and sacred, though it happens every day. Dawn is the child of God and darkness.* —Pawnee Prayer

## My Healing Words

November 12

*May we be nourished that we may nourish life.* —Ojai School

## My Healing Words

November 13

*For he is our God, and we are the people of his pasture and the sheep of his hand.* —Psalm 95:7 (RSV)

## My Healing Words

November 14

*Waking up this morning, I smile, twenty-four brand new hours are before me. I vow to live fully in each moment and to look at all beings with eyes of compassion.* —Thich Nhat Hanh

## My Healing Words

November 15

*Day arises from its sleep, day wakes up with the dawning light. Also you must arise, also you must awake, together with the day which comes.*
—Thule Eskimo Song

## My Healing Words

November 16

*Washing the dishes is like bathing a baby Buddha. The profane is the sacred. Everyday mind is Buddha's mind.* —Thich Nhat Hanh

## My Healing Words

November 17

*Let there be long breath and life.* —Arapaho Grace

## My Healing Words

November 18

*How excellent is thy loving-kindness, O God!* —Psalm 36:7 (ESV)

My Healing Words

November 19

*But still the hands of memory weave the blissful dreams of long ago.*
—George Cooper

## My Healing Words

November 20

*The sun has disappeared but I still know that your moon is there and your eyes and also your hands. Thus I am not afraid.* —Chanaian Christian Prayer

MY HEALING WORDS

November 21

*With humility, with awareness of the existence of life, and of the sufferings that are going on around us, let us pray for the establishment of peace in our hearts and on earth. Amen.* —Thich Nhat Hanh

MY HEALING WORDS

November 22

*My heart and my flesh sing joy to thee O God of life.* —Chinook Psalter

## My Healing Words

November 23

*May all things move and be moved in me and know and be known in me. May all creation dance for joy within me.* —Chinook Psalter

## My Healing Words

November 24

*Earth brings us into life and nourishes us. Earth takes us back again. Birth and death are present in every moment.* —Thich Nhat Hanh

## My Healing Words

November 25

*We are grateful for the food labored by many hands. May it give us strength, health and joy. May it increase our love.* —Unitarian Prayer

## My Healing Words

November 26

*I reverently speak in the presence of the Great Parent God: I give thee grateful thanks that Thou hast enabled me to live this day, the whole day in obedience to the excellent spirit of Thy ways.* —Shinto Evening Prayer

## My Healing Words

November 27

*It was the wind that gave them life. It is the wind that comes out of our mouths now that gives us life.* —Navajo Chant

## My Healing Words

November 28

*Great ones above and below, bless us, for we reach up to you.* —Chinook Psalter

## My Healing Words

November 29

*Put forth your hand and raise us up.* —Saint Hildegard of Bingen

## My Healing Words

November 30

*May we walk with grace and may the light of the universe shine upon our path.*
—Anonymous

## My Healing Words

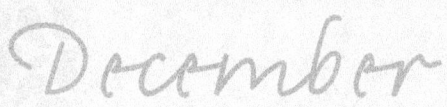

## Spiritual Discernment

Turn once, turn twice
Life's circular motion
spinning, spinning surrounded
by love and faith and hope

Gentle nudges from an inner voice
stop the cycle and propel us
forward if for a moment
we awaken to a new way, an open way

Like a feather we often drift
aimlessly, searching for the open way
that is ours
Often missing the meaning of the closed ways

Do not beat against the door of
the old and familiar
Waste not the energy to propel
us from the frantic circle
whirling and wanton misgivings
Dreams not realized

Take "us" out of the equation
Create a space for God to steer us
true and straight
with strength and fortitude

Go forth on our journey
unafraid, unencumbered
For life is not meant to live aimlessly
as an ambivalent bystander

Stand up, be proud, risk all
in the name of the one who gave you life
to live your life
completely and holy

Walk the path that is the right way
Your own unique way
paved with God's
love, enjoyment, surprise

For those who are willing to risk it all
Trust in him
Reap the rewards from now through
eternity

The prospect is not full of fear
but should abound in possibility, hope,
faith
Grasp at all that you know and
find comfort in
Seek out those who propel you forward
on your journey

Release yourself from the circular
stagnation
Relish your relationship with God
who knows you and loves you
Trust that he will send a messenger
to guide you always

Turn once, turn twice
Step out
Step forward
Live
Love
Let go

December 1

*Seek love in the pity of another's woe, in the gentle relief of another's care. In the darkness of night and the winter's snow. In the naked and outcast, seek love there.* —Anonymous

## My Healing Words

December 2

*Healing waters, you are the ones who bring us the life force. Help us to find nourishment so that we may look upon great joy.* —Hindu Prayer

## My Healing Words

December 3

*Create your own spiritual journey that weaves blasts of beauty, awe, love, pain, grief and loss into a mosaic of true self, rightness and hands of healing.*
—Martha W. Brandt

## My Healing Words

December 4

*Once we learn to touch this peace, we will be healed and transformed. It is not a matter of faith; it is a matter of practice.* —Thich Nhat Hanh

My Healing Words

December 5

*My child, be attentive to my words; incline your ear to my sayings. Do not let them escape from your sight; keep them within your heart. For they are life to those who find them, and healing to all their flesh.* —Proverbs 4:20–22 (NKJV)

## My Healing Words

December 6

*If you speak or act with a calm, bright heart, then happiness follows you, like a shadow that never leaves.* —Buddha

## My Healing Words

December 7

*And one of them, when he saw that he was healed, returned, and with a loud voice glorified God.* —Luke 17:15 (NKJV)

## My Healing Words

December 8

*This is the last world I shall make. I place it in your hands. Hold it in trust.*
—Jewish Prayer

## My Healing Words

December 9

*O Lord my God, I cried out to you for help and you healed me.*
—Psalm 30:2 (NKJV)

## My Healing Words

December 10

*Dear God, use my hands to heal the world so that we may live with compassion and loving-kindness.* —Venerable Master Chin Kung

## My Healing Words

December 11

*Purify the mind and heart to attain happiness. Be kind. Be compassionate.*
—Buddha

## My Healing Words

December 12

*Dear God, fill my heart with compassion that I may use gentle hands and kind words for those I love.* —Martha W. Brandt

## My Healing Words

December 13

*May you know how to look at yourself with the eyes of understanding and love.*
—Thich Nhat Hanh

## My Healing Words

December 14

*A generous heart, kind speech and a life of service and compassion are the things that renew humanity and can heal the world.* —Buddha

## My Healing Words

December 15

*Hold on to my hand, even if I have gone away from you.* —Pueblo Blessing

## My Healing Words

December 16

*Embrace the spirit of community and love today. Pay it forward by a gentle touch, a knowing look, a random act of kindness, a shared sadness or joy.*
—Martha W. Brandt

## My Healing Words

December 17

*God promises to make something good out of the storms that bring devastation to your life.* —Romans 8:28 (NKJV)

My Healing Words

December 18

*May all beings have happiness, and the causes of happiness.* —Buddhist Prayer

My Healing Words

December 19

*Be still and know that I am God.* —Psalm 46:10 (NKJV)

## My Healing Words

December 20

*A joy, a depression, a meanness, some momentary awareness comes as an unexpected visitor. Welcome and entertain them all! He may be clearing you out for some new delight.* —Rumi

## My Healing Words

December 21

*Our problems are solved by loving-kindness, by gentleness, by joy.* —Buddha

## My Healing Words

December 22

*Especially would we pray for those which minister to our sport or comfort that they may be treated with tenderness of hands, in thankfulness of heart, and that we may discover thee, the Creator, in all created things.*
—Traditional Christian Prayer

## My Healing Words

December 23

*Let your light shine before men, that they may see your good works and give glory to your Father who is in heaven.* —Matthew 5:16 (RSV)

## My Healing Words

December 24

*And one of them, when he saw that he was healed, returned, and with a loud voice glorified God.* —Luke 17:15 (NKJV)

## My Healing Words

December 25

*There is no need for suffering, God is here.* —Rumi

## My Healing Words

December 26

*Oh Great Spirit, I pray for myself in order that I may be healed.* —Navajo Prayer

## My Healing Words

December 27

*He sent his word and healed them, and delivered them from their destructions.*
—Psalms 107:20 (NKJV)

## My Healing Words

December 28

*All shall be well and all shall be well and all manner of things shall be well.*
—Blessed Julian of Norwich

## My Healing Words

December 29

*For I know the plans I have for you. . . . Plans to prosper you and not to harm you, plans to give you hope and a future.* —Jeremiah 29:11 (NKJV)

## My Healing Words

December 30

*When you talk, you are only repeating what you already know. But if you listen, you may learn something new.* —Dalai Lama

## My Healing Words

December 31

*Dear God, on this glorious morning you have made, what can I do today to help someone else? How can I be a blessing and use my hands of healing for someone else?* —Martha W. Brandt

## My Healing Words

## Acknowledgements

First and foremost, I would like to express my deep appreciation for my parents Roger Choate Wonson and Mary Sue Littlejohn Wonson for their enduring love and support. At 93 and 96, respectively, they will find comfort in this book having lost a daughter at the young age of 60. I am particularly grateful to my grandmother, Agnes May Choate Wonson, who instilled a love of poetry when I first began writing at age 12. I am also thankful to my great aunt, Martha Taylor Wonson, who quoted poetry to me many a sleepless night in my youth! I am thankful for the inspiration, interest, and encouragement from my husband of 33 years, David, and my three wonderful adult children: David Rufus Choate Brandt, Karlsen Taylor Brandt, and Mary Catharine Brandt. Thank you to all my friends and family for your inspiration and guidance. I am dedicating this book to my dear sister, Karen May Wonson Stearns (DeeDee), whom I miss everyday and who has inspired many of the poems in this book. I write knowing she is still a strong influence in my creativity and her spirit will continue to support and guide me.

## About the Author

Martha W. Brandt is a wife, mother, and an award-winning poet. Her work can be found in *Wee Wisdom Children's Magazine* (1973), the *National Library of Poetry* (1997-1998), and her self-published book *Poetry for the Spiritual Soul* (2008). In 2011, Brandt received the second-place award in the Eber and Wein Publishing contest for her poem "Tuition, Taxes and Time." Her poem "The Time Between" received an honorable mention in the Eber and Wein Publishing National Amateur Poetry Competition and was published in *American Poet: Volume 4* (2016). "Sojourn at Autumn Dawn" was published in the *Eber & Wein Best Poets of 2016: Volume 3*. Her short story "Dream Baby" is featured in *Our Children Live On: Miraculous Moments for the Bereaved* by Elissa Al-Chokhachy. In 2011, she was the selected poet for the Improbable Places Poetry Tour with the Montserrat College of Art.

Martha has an engineering background from Bates College and the Massachusetts Institute of Technology, but her true passion is writing children's stories, inspirational stories, and poetry. Martha enjoys running, raising funds as a Kids at Heart Marathon Team member for Boston Children's Hospital (Boston Marathon 2003), singing, playing piano, and crocheting prayer shawls. She is an avid participant in Family Promise, a local outreach program for homeless families on the North Shore of Boston. She grew up in Beverly, Massachusetts, and is the mother to three grown children. She still resides in Beverly with her husband, David, and their new babies—two Great Danes! Martha is currently employed as a Senior Quality Engineer with IXYS Integrated Circuits Division.

My Healing Words

My Healing Words

My Healing Words

## My Healing Words

My Healing Words